Death Friend

Yvonne Woodland

chipmunkapublishing
the mental health publisher

Yvonne Woodland

Published by
Chipmunkapublishing
PO Box 6872
Brentwood
Essex CM13 1ZT
United Kingdom

http://www.chipmunkapublishing.com

Edited by Marc Wilson

Chipmunkapublishing gratefully acknowledge the support of Arts Council England.

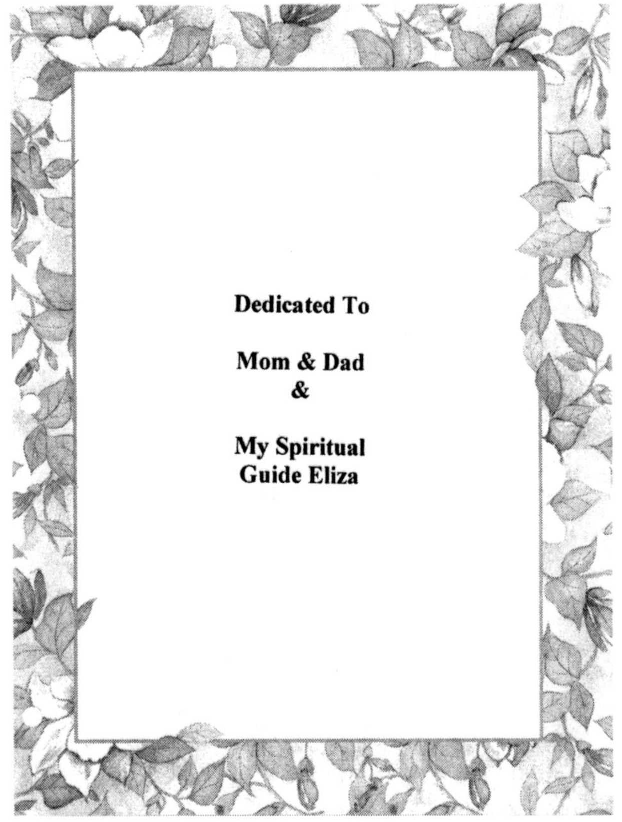

Dedicated To

Mom & Dad
&

My Spiritual
Guide Eliza

Yvonne Woodland

Contents Page

Yvonne Woodland

DEATH FRIEND

After years of dreaded darkness, into the bright light.

I was first hospitalised at the age of 38. Looking back on my life, I would like to tell you a little about it.

Yvonne Woodland

FAMILY DYNAMICS

My father was born December 1, 1904 in England. My Mother was born July 22, 1918 in Stockholm, Sk. They were married September 12, 1939. My father had a son from a previous marriage; he was born August 18, 1934. My father was widowed from his first wife.

My brother was born December 7, 1940. I was born March 29, 1942. My mother was pregnant with twins in 1946, one was stillborn and the other had died and was decaying inside her. The problem was corrected; my next brother was born July 10, 1947. My sister was born June 24, 1951, and brother born October 18, 1955, followed by another brother November 22, 1957 and my last sister born June 8, 1959. So all and all there were eight of us kids.

CHILDS PLAY

I was born in St. Thomas, ON., March 29, 1942 in an Air Force Base hospital as my father was in the Air Force. He was a chef who would cook for the officers. As far back as I can remember, which would have to be three, which was in Stockhohm, Sk., my grandfather would give me raisins on a piece of newspaper, that was a real treat. I must have been my grandfather's favourite. Upon his death, I received an inheritance of $56.00, which I bought my first bicycle with and I was about eight at that time.

I have pictures of my brother and myself and I had two big dolls, which I played with very often and I brought them out to B.C. at the age of four.

We lived in Surrey for many years and growing up I played with many a mud pies. Mom would give me baking soda or baking powder and I would make cookies with it and set them out in the sun and they would bake and rise, I certainly never ate them.

In those days we had a wood stove, there was lots of wood around to make wooden dolls. Take a block of wood, put a cross board for arms, boards for legs. The hair was made from twine, which we frayed and curled. Or we would use curly woods shavings from a wood plane or steel curly shavings from a lathe, which was nailed on with staple nails. We were certainly handy with a hammer and nails. The wooden dolls were always dressed in baby clothes, from shoes to hats. We had a wonderful time playing with those dolls. I had paper dolls also, but I didn't play very long with them.

The two dolls I brought from Sk, were made of cloth and had plastic arms and legs. I always wanted a boy doll, so I found a pair of my dad's underwear and I proceeded to cut and sew a little penis and two testicles and I attached them onto one of the dolls. There I had a boy doll! I could dress him like a little boy. He would have a twin sister. When I got a little bit older, I had to be in grade 4 or 5, we would take our pen tops and pretend they were little people and we would make paper clothes for them. We were always using our scissors and designing different patterns and colouring them with crayons

I had one girl friend that we would play house in the chicken house with the chickens being our children. Or we would play house with the geese or the goats, boy they were very cranky creatures. Some times we would play with grasshoppers, wrap them in Kleenex, they always made a mess of the Kleenex. We always had a lot of fun pretending.

NAUGHTY

My brother was fourteen months older than I was. When we were six and seven, we would get on the running board of the egg truck and go for a ride down the street. One day, my brother jumped off and he made into the ditch all right, when I jumped off, my right foot got caught under the back wheel of the truck. I went home and told my mother that a big rock had fallen on it, and to this day I think she believed me. I didn't do much playing for a couple of days after that. We never rode the running board of the egg truck again.

I was about 5 or 6 and I peed in the grass only 10 feet away from the outhouse and my mother saw me do it. She said I was lazy so she took the willow switch to me once. I don't remember ever getting it again.

When I was about eight, my friend and I walked four miles to the drug store; we proceeded to steal a chocolate bar. We were caught red handed. I was so scared I almost peed my pants. I remember asking the man where the bathroom was. He told us he was going to tell our mothers and he let us go. During our walk home along the main highway, we would get down on our knees on the side of the main highway and we prayed to God, the man in the drug store wouldn't tell our mothers. My friend was from a very religious family, and I had a lot of religious upbringing. We were very scared of what would happen to us. We were pretty lucky as we never heard anything about that incident. We certainly never attempted to do that again.

My mother never put up with sassy behaviour, I was about twelve years old and I was being sassy and called her "dearie." I got smacked in the mouth for that. Never did anything like that again either.

KIDS ENTERTAINMENT

The neighbour up the street was the first to get a television, which all the neighbourhood kids would go for a couple of hours a few nights a week. We would watch all the old westerns. The mother that had the television liked Liberace, so we always had to watch him. That didn't last to long as we finally got our own television.

The neighbourhood kids would get together and put on plays for the parents and anybody that wanted to watch us. We would do plays like Rumpelstiltskin. It was a lot of fun gather all the props and studying the lines, then performing for everyone.

We would always ride bikes, wherever we went; swimming at the pool three miles away was always a good daytime exercise.

We lived by a big hill, so in the winter time when it snowed we would sleigh ride for hours. We would either make our sleds or use an inner tube. One year for Christmas I got a new store bought sled. That was a thrill.

Another thing we did, as we got a little older we would get our blanket and pillow and go down to the drive in theatre and lie on the ground under the big screen and watch the movies. They usually had two movies. This was in the summer time and we would get home very late.

MONEY MAKERS

We were always trying to make money, whether it was by stripping cascara bark from the trees or collecting pop and beer bottles. I had a paper route, which I started at about the age of eight. I had it for a number of years. I learned to collect money, make change and deliver the papers on my bicycle, which had a big carrier on it.

When I got a little bit older in the summer time I would pick strawberries and gooseberries. We had a lot of strawberry fights in the patch. We always had our shirts and shorts stained with strawberry stains. We made money at picking them too. When strawberries and gooseberries were done we would get on the back of a big truck and head to the bean fields and pick beans.
In high school I worked in a café for awhile, I did a lot of baby sitting for the neighbours. Then, at seventeen, I worked at the cannery, which they were doing beans and peas and earned money for clothes for school. It was sure fun to shop.

Growing up then, there was no such thing as allowance. We always had to earn our spending money, as it was very tight budget we lived on. We always had food on the table and clothes on our back which were hand me downs mostly. I don't think we were hard done by though.

CHORES

My first chore was to go one and a half miles down the road on my bicycle and get two quarts of milk every day. I had a backpack that would fit the two quarts very nicely. A couple of times I fell off my bicycle and of course broke the two quarts of milk. It was very costly, but I don't remember getting into trouble over it.

Coming from a big family there was always lots of dishes to do. I would either wash or dry; that was a nightly chore.

I was nine years old when my sister was born. I remember the night that it happened. When she was about two I would take her wherever I went. I would carry her on my hip. My girlfriend had a brother about the same age and she had to take him with her too. We played for hours with my sister and her brother on our hips. Maybe that is why I have big hips today.

When I got older and we got our first lawn mover, I would mow the grass, which we had a fair amount of it. One day mowing the grass in my bare feet, as we always ran in the summer, I ran into a snake down in the ditch. The snake bit my big toe, so I chewed the snake up with the lawn mower. I liked to mow the lawn, so I did it many of times and did a good job of it.

CHILDHOOD ABUSE

The neighbourhood was full of boys and not girls. I usually hung out with my brother and his friends. When the boys got tired of me hanging around with them, and they were going down the gravel road to places that they didn't want me along, they would push me down on the road and I would always have knees that looked like hamburger. I always went home crying.

One day, when I was delivering my papers, one of my customer's kids was playing cowboys and he had a lasso. He must have been a damn good shot, as he lassoed me around the neck and pulled me off my bike. I had a dandy rope burn around my neck. Many scrapes and bruises too.

Many of times while delivering my papers I would run into creeps in their cars. They would call me over and ask the time or direction to places. I would go up to the car and the creep would be jacking off. I would quickly get away from the car and go on doing my papers and I would tell my mother about the incident, when I got home. At that time, nothing seemed to be done about such things.

When I was about eleven or twelve, a new girl moved into the neighbourhood and we became friends. Her father was a very mean and vicious man. He would use the razor strap on her every time he thought she deserved it, whether it was because she didn't carry in the sawdust for the sawdust hopper on the stove or any other minor thing. She always had welts on her arms and back from the strap, which really was ugly looking. He would also have sex with her at night. I always wondered what was wrong with her mother to allow such things to happen to her.

When this girlfriend and I would take a walk up the street to see other friends, there was a man that would see us coming and he would go into his garage, which had a big window and he would jack off. We would run away as fast as we could go.

TOMBOY

With people having more property then, there was a lot more woods. We were always playing in them. There was a creek, wild flower (Trilliums and bleeding hearts) growing all over the place, lots of stumps, ferns, moss, which was my favourite thing to play with. Fungus that we would take and write on them. Trees were plentiful so we would be always climbing them. The creek was the most fun, building dams and rafts to sail from one side to the other. Many gum boots full of water that is for sure.

Blackberry bushes were fun to tunnel under the foliage and make a house in them, I played house for hours with the wooden dolls. I made a lot of different rooms, so it was like a playhouse.

We played cowboys and Indians very often with our toy guns and bows and arrows, we would make from branches from the woods. We always had are own jack knives. The Indians would have a full head dress with feathers; we got from the chicken house. I remember being socked in the nose playing that, which was very painful and bloody. My brother and a few boys from the neighbourhood built a two story fort, they, of course, were the cowboys.

We were always playing warriors, when the brackens were in season. We would pull them out of the ground and remove the foliage from them and use them as spears. We would make shields out of plywood or we would use garbage can lids. It is a wonder we didn't put somebody's eye out.

Us, kids were always building something. We would make stilts. My first stilts were two jam cans with ropes for my hands, which were attached to the cans. Then I graduated to wooden stilts, which I made myself out of two by fours and hammer and nails. The neighbourhood kids would all walk down the road on theirs. Tall People we were!

We would play outside when it was dark; our favourite game was called "Whistle or Cry". It is like tag, but it is played in the dark and the person that was it, would call out whistle or cry. We would all give out either and then they would proceed to find us.

We were always building fires to cook what our mothers gave us, which was usually potatoes or we would go to the orchard and get apples off the tree and roast them.

We played baseball in the cow pasture. Something else we did in the cow pasture was, we would join hands and one person would take hold of the electric barbwire fence that was to keep the cows in, and the one on the end would get the shock. That was really dumb, but boy was that fun. Sometimes we would go and lick the block of salt that was for the cows.

When we got a little bit older the neighbourhood boys built a swing from a tree that had a tire on the end of the rope. They built a twenty foot high platform to climb up and then get on the tire rope and swing through the clearing.

The great excitement for the neighbourhood kids was when Mom would chop the head off of a chicken and let it go and the chicken would run all over the place until the nerves would stop. We put the chicken in boiling water to take the feathers off, then gut it and see all the body parts and the unlayed eggs. It was pretty stinky, but supper was sure great. Our neighbour would slaughter his cow and let us kids of the neighbourhood watch, what a sight that was. He would never let us see him kill the cow.

My brother and the neighbourhood boys and myself would go down to the river when the ooligans were running and get a bucket or two of ooligans and bring them home to Mom. She would clean them and then fry them up for us. What a feast and really tasty.

RELIGIOUS TRAINING

I started to go to Sunday school at about the age of six. I would walk to the corner and an old school bus would pick us kids up and drive about four miles to the church. I went for about two years taking my nickel, which was a lot of money for our family to spare at the time, but that was all we could afford. I would put my nickel in my collection envelope and put it into the collection plate faithfully every Sunday. My mom informed me that the church said that was not enough and we would have to give more. That was the end of the Sunday school for me; my mom wouldn't let me go back to that church. They weren't interested in teaching children about God or the Bible, just how much money they collected from you.

Then I started to go to Sunday school with some friends of my mom and dad, they had two daughters about the same age as I was. I would stay with them over the weekend and go on Sundays that lasted a couple of years.

I went to Bible Camp a number of times and I always had a good time, it was a lot of fun. There was always swimming, hiking, nature finds, treasure hunts, wiener and marshmallow roasts and then there was Bible studies. When I was about twelve, my stepbrother, which he is eight years older than I am, got involved with a church he would preach the gospel. He would also sing with a couple of other people in the church and they sounded so good. He was also good at yodeling. I went to Sunday school and church with him. There would be Bible school in the summertime for us kids and always a Sunday school picnic. The picnic was always a lot of fun with games and sports. Always Ice Cream!

One summer there was a giant tent put up in a middle of a cow pasture and they had a revival meeting for a whole week. I would go and loved to sing the hymns.

Then I stopped going to church for a while. Then I started to go with my brother and his girlfriend and I was baptized in the Anglican Church, which was our faith in the first place. When my future husband to be and I were getting married, our bands were read for three consecutive weeks before the marriage took place. We were married in the Anglican Church and our three children were christened there also. We didn't go to church after we were married. I go to church in spurts now, but I don't think to be a good Christian that you have to go to church on Sundays, you can be one everyday of the week. Dealing with a lot of people that go to church every Sunday, I find them to be very hypocritical.

SPECIAL OCCASIONS

As far back as I can remember it was my fifth birthday. My mom had a birthday party for me and invited all the neighbour kids. I remember getting a plastic green toy telephone from the boy down the street. As soon as I opened it, he said that it was his and I couldn't have it. He took it and played with it until he forgot about it and then my mom put it away until later for me.

My mom would make a birthday cake and she always would wrap a penny in wax paper and insert it in the cake, the lucky one that got it was thrilled.

Valentine days was always special as I always had valentine cards to give my friends. The teacher would make a colourful box for the valentine and on that day she would open it and hand out all the cards.

My mom would always make a heart shaped cake for us for dessert that night. Nicely decorated with cinnamon hearts and lot of icing.

Easter was special too. We would get a big Easter basket with one large chocolate egg in it, which was nicely decorated and had our names on them, plus other colourful candy Easter eggs. We always coloured eggs that my mom would boil up for us, we would either paint or put stickers on them. Mom would always make a cake, eventually she got to the point of making a cake that looked like a Easter bunny. We would always have Easter dinner with all the family, which was always very nice.

Halloween was a lot of fun for us kids as we would always dress up. It was usually like a bum; charcoaled faces, old hats and raggy clothes. We would take our pillow case and go door to door, singing out trick or treat. Our favourite item was homemade candy apples and fudge. We got a lot of candy kisses and suckers, so we always had a feast. The older kids would push over the out houses and throw rotten eggs at things, but us little kids would just have fun dressing up and going door to door.

Next was Christmas, which was a very special event in our household. My dad always bought the presents and made sure we got what we had asked for within reason. Whatever he could afford and I am sure he would pay the next year for it all.

Mom would do the cooking and cleaning for Christmas, decorating the house and of course put up the tree, which I helped decorate. I would make red and green paper chains or string popcorn to put on the tree. Mom was well known for her cinnamon buns and cookies. My dad being a chef would help with Christmas dinner; he would always look after the turkey and would carve it. He always made Christmas cakes for the family. As we got older and the family grew, to many of us Christmas just seemed to get more exciting. That went on for many years until mom and dad could not do it anymore. Now it is our turn.

My dad passed away in October 1986 and my mother in December 1999.

TEENAGER

I got my last doll for my thirteenth birthday. I just about didn't get it as my mom left it in a store. When she went back it was still there. It worked out OK in the end.

I always would dream of snakes around my bed when I was about fourteen. Or, I would start to cry for no reason at all. My mom would let me cry, I guess she figured it was just apart of growing up. My older brothers were not very supportive, as they would always pick on me by punching me in the arm or by calling me the buzz-beer kid. Meaning I was now wearing a bra.

My first serious love boyfriend situation began when I was fifteen. I was madly in love with this boy. Emotions ran very high and lot of things happened. We had a good summer, swimming and going on car rallies.

Then he started to get mean and I was in tears. Next thing I knew, he had a new girlfriend. I was devastated, I couldn't eat, sleep and I cried all the time. I lost a lot of weight, I had no energy. I remember trying to climb the stairs at school; it took all the energy I had to get to the top. Then the ribbing and ridicule started by his new girlfriend and her friend. He was not decent enough to keep things to himself. Everybody knew what had transpired between us. There was a lot of psychological damage done. So you know what was coming at me all the time. There were boys calling my mom and telling her that they wanted to do you know what, to me.

I did not enjoy my teenage years and I found I did not have too many friends. I dated a few more boys. I found that my brother and his friends were not supportive.

I did not do to well in high school with all the bullying that was going on. The only class I did well in was shorthand. I got straight A's, probably because I have a good memory.

My mom was pregnant with my youngest sister and she was having problems and was put to bed. I had to quit high school and look after the house and the rest of the family. Once my mom had my sister, everything was going well, I went to commercial college for six months taking commercial courses.

I was going to join the Air Force and took the tests for it. All I had to do was go for a medical. As a teenager I always wanted to be a police woman, so that was the best thing to do was to join the Air Force. Then I met my husband to be. We bought a new three bedroom house two months later and we were married in three months. I worked for a year and a half and then became pregnant which then I quit working and became a housewife.

LIFE AS A HOUSEWIFE

Life of a housewife was always very busy with cooking, baking and cleaning house. I enjoyed sewing for the kids when they were young, sewing for the house like drapery and slipcovers for the chair and chesterfield. I did sewing for my mother, clothes for the special occasions like her birthday or mother's day or Christmas. She always loved that, getting new clothes. In the summertime there was canning and freezing of fruits and vegtables or making jams and jellies. Of course, there was always budgeting of the money my husband gave me for the house and everything else that I would like to have, within reason.

When I was pregnant, my husband was not very supportive, he messed with other women, it was like he didn't like the responsibility of having a child or having something wrong with that child, as he told my mother that if there was something wrong with it, it was not coming home. As I was pregnant three times in three years it was very difficult and trying on me, and made me very angry. We made it through those times and had three beautiful children.

Through the years I took some night school courses, like exercise, upholstery, baking, resin craft, shorthand and bookkeeping. I did bowl twice a week and played softball, which I really enjoyed and the kids did too. There was always gardening to do which I like to make flower beds and rockeries, I thought nothing of moving ten yards of mushroom manure or top soil to the vegetable garden and of course, to my flowers gardens, which was always very colourful and showy. I like to crochet, which I made many things like dresses and blanket and afghans to novelties and doll clothes. My husband and I took ballroom dancing in night school and we did a lot of dancing.

In 1969, my mother-in-law moved in with us. She was very elderly and my children were very young and that didn't work out to well. That was a real trying time in my life. We moved down to her house at the beach and sold the house we had purchase in 1960. I did get a vehicle at that time and was able to go more places, whether it was to take her to the doctor or the kids to school and shopping with my mother, as she was my best friend. My sister was very young at that time and my three kids played a lot with her. I was always a taxi.

My mother-in law passed away and we inherited the house, which we were badly in need of to remodel the house. We started to remodel as soon as the money dictated it. It took many years and it was not finished when I left there. There was digging out of a partial basement which I did. It was pure gravel. Tearing down walls and porches to mixing cement with the electric cement mixer .I was always painting or wallpapering. You can see that I was a very active woman.

Money was tight so there were no allowances for the kids. They had paper routes and/or babysat when they became of age. The kids were either in bowling baseball or soccer, which was always a busy time taking them to their sports. They all graduated from high school which I was very please and moved away from home at a early age.

NON EARLY INTERVENTION

I was first hospitalized at the age of 38. Looking back on my life as a teenager, things were not very good. I got through a lot of it; I married at the age of 18 and had my first child at 20. In three years, less a day, I had 3 children.

With an amount of marital problems through the years, we struggled. I was so angry with my husband that I literally saw red. Being that angry and not venting it, I found it very stressful and it probably is the reason that I had a lot of stomach problems (repressed anger and/or depression). I went to my General Practitioner many times complaining of stomach problems and he could never find anything wrong. Then morbidity set in, I thought I was going to die and my children would not have a mother to care for them and that was very stressful. After a number of years of that, I finally got passed it.

I went to work once my children were old enough to fend for themselves a little bit more. Money was tight and the kids needed more clothing and then there was more food to put on the table. The first job I had was very stressful and it didn't last to long. Then I got on to doing Insurance and I enjoyed it very much and was doing woell. Then I got mixed up with the wrong people, things started to go downhill. I got mixed up with a fellow and then the bottom dropped out. I had to quit my job and my marriage came apart. My husband said I had to get out and out on the street I went.

Death Friend

Prior to being out on the street, my general practitioner sent me to see a Psychiatrist, my paranoia became increasingly worse, as I have had some paranoia all my life but was able to control it as I did with many things. The first Psychiatrist, I only told him what I wanted him to hear; it was not a good relationship. I went to a second Psychiatrist, who treated it as a family dynamics issue and wanted me to blame my mother. There was no way I was going to do that. So that was the end of that Psychiatrist, I would not go back.

As time went on, a lot of things began to happen, things became very unreal. My girlfriend, who lived down the street, always told me how unreal I was even before my psychoses hit. She was a psych-nurse. She would tell my son that it was not right, as he would go down and tell her what I was doing, either I was crying or sleeping all day ,but she did nothing about it.

I thought the telephones were bugged and I told my husband about my fears and he told me I was crazy. That was the worse thing he could have told me, as I just clamed up and wouldn't tell anybody what I was feeling or thinking or anything that was going on in my life. The paranoia and the psychoses, made the horror more intense and the matter worse. I started to sleep a lot and cry. I think I slept and cried for a year, my body just shut down. Many trips in tears to my general practitioner at this time were not fruitful. Years later, he told me he didn't know what to do with me, so he chose to do nothing, but he was happy that something had been done.

PSYCHOSIS

With all the things happening, like thinking the satellites were spying on me. The radio and television, I thought were talking directly to me. Thought broadcasting and people monitoring me is a big one. People would smile, frown, laugh and say things that were a special message for me, as it meant something. When I read certain books, words jump out at me. Names, colours and numbers have special meaning to me. My mind is always calculating numbers, whether it be license plates, house and street numbers or what I spent in the grocery store. Reading the shapes of the clouds, I get the dictionary out or other books that I have relating to what I see. My brain is always racing in one direction or another. Synchronicity is a big aspect of it also. Carl Jung's theory, I can relate and understand it a lot. Persecution is also a big part in the psychoses.

I get pains in my hands like Christ's nails and what makes sense to myself, is that it is a Spiritual Emergence, with the religious upbringing that I had. I am always questioning myself. When in psychosis, I think I am the Virgin Mary. I was told later, that stems from being separated from my children and not being able to nurture them. I thought was going to have twins, a girl and a boy, which would bring equality to this world. I remember asking if I was "special", I certainly got a sharp and snapping answer "NO". This was never a topic of discussion – just more confusion. The hell

of psychosis and the hell of reality are just about
the same.

Death Friend

HOSPITALIZATION

September 30, 1979, I had to be out of the house. I had no job, very little money and no place to go. We had a tent trailer in our yard without licence plates on it, so I licensed the tent trailer and went down to the campgrounds and camped, as sick as I was. The weather was very cold and I got sick because of it. I would go and see my children every day as I could not take them with me. I wanted them to have a home and three meals a day. I, at that time, could not supply them with that. Things were very bad, one day my mother told me I could not live like that, so for me to come to her home and stay there. She fed me well and let me sleep and cry all I wanted and with that I gained a lot of weight. People would say things to me that I took offence to, so then I would get in my car and drive from one part of the city to the other end and back, all the time I would be crying my eyes out, which was a dumb thing to do.

I would always end up where my children were. Tired and cold, they would always send me back to my mom's. Then things got really ugly and I said something to my children that was very disturbing, upsetting and heart breaking to them. They were smart enough to know that it was not normal behaviour for their mother. They in turn told my brothers. They are all six feet tall strapping men and how do you argue with that. They packed me off to Riverview. My mother was just in tears and she made sure that she fed me before they took me.

I was admitted to Riverview; they bath me, even though I had had a shower and curled my hair before they took me, not knowing what was going to happen. The doctors in Riverview stripped searched me, I might be guilty of many things but doing drugs is certainly not one of them, they could have at least talked to my family before doing that, as I was very humiliated by it. Then I was locked up. As bad as it was, something had to be done because I could not go on like I was. I was put on a medication called Fluphenazine, this medication cured one monster, but created another.

My mom, dad and my sister and her new baby would come and visit me every second day, my children would come in twice a week to see me, so I had a lot of visitors. The Clergy in there told me "once a mental patient always a mental patient", otherwise telling me there was no hope, which in my opinion is pretty stupid. You put up with a lot of negativity. I kept to my self a lot, doing crossword puzzles or crocheting, which I did two afghans and a blanket. The blanket is still on my bed after 28 years. I had a little job in their payroll department, counting out money for the patients for the little jobs that they did.

Two months later I was discharged as they said I was doing well. Before my discharge, my family was brought in to a family conference. It was really funny to see Mom, Dad, brothers and sisters and their spouses coming in, it was like a little army had hit. I was not allowed in on the conference, so I have no idea what was said or what my diagnoses was, until after my discharge I asked my mother what was wrong with me, she informed me that I had a chemical imbalance.

Next time I saw my mental health worker I asked her about the diagnoses and she said, my brain does not make a certain chemical. I was getting medication, so I thought that would solve the problem, figured this was just normal, not told about side effects from the medication. My sister-in-law was a psych-nurse, also, but nothing was discussed in front of my family or myself. I was in the dark along with my family regarding mental illness.

For the next seven years, all I wanted to do was die. Life was not worth living. Death just seemed to be the best friend I could have had, all I wanted to do was self destruct, but I couldn't do that to my family, so sleep was the only freedom I knew. I had absolutely no energy, no energy even to talk. I would sleep 20 hours a day and then ask for sleeping pills, so I could sleep the other 4 hours, that's how much I enjoyed life. One night, I saw a very bright light when I was sleeping, which I put down to a near death experience. There was physical evidence of this as I had sore eyes for many days after. That was the turning point from my hell, things started to get better after that. That light was sure bright, I certainly believe in a Supreme Higher Power.

Picture drawn in hospital as an exercise when I was very ill.

FENDING FOR MYSELF

My mental health worker told me to go out and get a job and an apartment. Never asked what my financial picture was. Basically fend for yourself! In the next breath, I was told that she would not hire me! If she would not hire me then who would ever hire me? I did go out and got a job paying very little money, certainly not enough to get an apartment with. It was a real struggle and very painful as all I wanted to do was stay at home and sleep. I lasted 5 months on that job, long enough to collect UI, so I would have money for the essentials and I could sleep, pushing from my family and myself, I managed to get other jobs, but the same scenario was happening.

I dated a fellow in 1981 for 3 years. He was a likeable fellow, very soft and cuddly. I liked him a lot and he took me across a lot of rocky roads, which I was thankful for. We went for dinners and a lot of movies. Never knew what the movies were about, because I always slept through them all.

I did have a reprieve in 1984, when the doctor said I was doing well and took me off the medication. I felt wonderful for a number of months; I was working, making more money so that I could afford an apartment. I lost all the weight that I had gained and I enjoyed my independence. It didn't last to long as I got ill again and was hospitalized for 3 weeks and put on the same medication as before. I changed Health Regions; reason was my change of address. At this point I was not working again due to illness and back to feeling dreadfully awful.

Finally, in 1987 I asked my doctor if there was any other medication I could try, he changed my medication to Fluanxol and said that it wasn't as depressing as Fluephenazine. At that point I could have choked him! After all the years of misery. Once the new medication got into my system, I looked forward to the mornings and days, life was worth living again. I got another job in Vancouver, which I really liked and did well at it, that was in 1986. I moved out of my apartment and moved in with my daughter and husband as they were struggling to make ends meet, it was beneficial to both of us. Health Region changed again. In 1989, the management changed on the job and I was wrongfully dismissed.

In 1985, I started dating again. Life was going OK. There were a lot of positive things and events in my life, which I appreciated and was thankful for too. For a person with mental illness, it is an important part of life and a plus to have a partner – someone to be intimate with, do things and go places with together. In 1988, I moved in with him and life was going OK, as I was working and he had his own business. In 1991, I was working again and the job was very stressful. I hung in there until 1995. Due to downsizing, I was unemployed again. I moved out of living with my boyfriend as we found we could not live together. We just carried on a relationship after that, and it seemed to work better.

EDUCATION

In 1994, I went to a mental health seminar called "People living with people with Schizophrenia" Boy! Did I see myself, a lot of the symptoms and information that I received from the seminar. I went to my mental health worker and asked her if I have Schizophrenia, she said "yes, don't you know?" One Health Region just assumed I knew from my first hospitalization. Chemical imbalance doesn't tell me anything. Diabetes is a chemical imbalance too, but they don't tell people with Diabetes that, so why tell me that. I didn't know what I was dealing with. Maybe there would not have been the wasted years of a good life. WASTE, WASTE, WASTE!!! I CANNOT THINK OF A MORE DYNAMNIC WORD FOR IT.

In 1994, approximately, I heard about Prozac and the different effects and side effects. I asked my mental health worker about this, she said I didn't need it. I asked my doctor and he prescribed it for me. Prozac gives me confidence and energy to make life better. People and my family say what a difference it made to me. It brings out the anger in me so I can vent my feeling and be more assertive.

In 1994, I met Marge Delange, Regional Co-ordinator for BCSS. She got me involved with the Partnership Education Program, going to schools, colleges, Justice Institute, hospitals and many other educational centres. Partnership Program consists of a Professional, family member and a consumer telling their personal stories and answering question about their experience with mental illness to faculty and students. I was involved with puppetry, educating elementary school students about Schizophrenia. I did some TV videos in Sechelt and Delta, B.C. With the education I was doing, I was also getting educated along with my family, which was a huge plus.

I had the opportunity to take the Journey of Hope Family Educational program, which lead me the BRIDGES program out of Tennessee. I was very excited about it, that I proceeded to bring it to the Province along with Al Matthews and Marge Delange. Everyone being diagnosed with mental illness should take the program. Doctors should recommend that their clients get the information they need when faced with their illness. Getting funding for the program was not pleasant, a lot of negativity, but we did and it is here. Hopefully other lives won't have the wasted years.

In 1999, I had another period of psychoses and I changed doctors, we tried some of the newer medications and another older one but they did not agree with me. Insisting that I be put back on Fluanxol, I am back on track and doing well. My mind is at rest now.

EDUCATION, MEDICATION, FAMILY AND FRIENDS. All very important. I have a lot of support from my family and friends and especially from my children. They say I HAVE BEEN TO HELL AND BACK!

ELDEST DAUGHTER'S STORY

As children, if mom had signs of this illness they were not visible to us as life carried on normally. We went to school, generally mom drove us each day and picked us up after school, even in high school and after school we played with our friends. We played team sports and had paper routes and babysat. Families on the street where we lived got together on weekends for drinks/dinners, hot dog/marshmallow roasts at the beach. We slept over at each others homes, and all kids played together regardless of age.

In my early teens, Mom showed signs of being depressed, but at the time we figured it was because our parents were openly showing signs of discord in their marriage. By this time they were married at least 15 years.

Slowly the illness took over and mom stopped getting up and driving us to school, stopped being concerned about the way she looked and just sat at home crying. Again as kids we figured this was because of our parents dying relationship. You would think that having an aunt and a family friend who were psychiatric nurses that these early symptoms would be noticed and brought to someone's attention.

With their relationship over, Mom moved out and sunk deeper and deeper into depression and the symptoms of schizophrenia taking over. When we would visit her at our grandparents 2 – 3 times a week. Chances are she was sleeping when we got there, she wasn't good company, and we didn't stay long. She slept most days away. My grandmother would feed her well and consequently she gained a lot of weight. Due to some drawings / writings mom was doing on a pad of paper, our aunt realized the state mom was in and finally a family intervention and psychiatric hospitalization. This whole process took about 3 years!!

At this time I was 16 years old and grew up fast. I was now the mother figure to my siblings. My brother, sister and I would drive from White Rock to Coquitlam to visit mom at Riverview Hospital. 2 – 3 times a week. Fortunately this only lasted 4 – 6 months and mom was released and was back living at her parent's home in Aldergrove. She would come to see us during the week after school and we would visit her at our grandparents on Sundays for Sunday dinner. She eventually was well enough to work. She worked for her brother painting apartments and eventually moved out on her own to an apartment in Burnaby. I was also living in Burnaby, but involved in my own life, working, boyfriend, weekends away, etc and mom worked long days and then would come home and sleep. She was still suffering silently.

Over the years she would relapse again, couldn't work so couldn't afford to live on her own, eventually moved in with my sister and her husband and my brother, who all shared a house in Surrey. Again, she recovered and went back to work and had a life of relative normality. I now have a family of my own. Mom moved in with us in March 1995. When she moved in my kids were 3 & 4 years old. I worked part-time and when my daughter started school in September 1995 it was nice having someone to pick her up from school and watch my son. I have really appreciated having my mom to help me out all these years and am very grateful to her.

At the writing of this October 2008, Mom still lives with us, my daughter has just started attending UBC taking psychology courses and my son is finishing grade 12. Both kids have benefited from having her live with us. My husband and I have benefited from having her live with us. Mom has benefited from living with us. She has relapsed a few times since she has lived with us. Her psychiatrist, Dr L. has been a godsend. He has tried to find the right meds for her. In the beginning he tried the newer meds, but eventually going back to her old standby when the newer ones disagreed with her system.

Mom continues to suffer from depression. Whether caused by guilt (she is very hard on herself), her weight, a run of bad weather or a long winter, a cold/cough that won't go away, these things bring her down. It is hard to motivate her. She sits all day looking/staring out the window, drinking her coffee, water or pop. She used to do most of the housework, but that has dwindled down to doing laundry. Her schizophrenia has been under control again but the depression continues somewhat. She has her days. Mom looks forward to Christmas each year, flowers in the spring, warm summer weather and travelling. She would still like to visit China, take an Alaskan cruise and a Mediterranean cruise.

Since the loss of her boyfriend last year, she is trying to establish friendships with others. She has met and become friends with Linda, Paul and Annette. She continues to have a best friend in Marge. She met Marge 20 years ago at a workshop for people with schizophrenia. Marge was working for BCSS. They were doing the Partnership Program together. They gave talks, seminars, puppet shows to university psych students, elementary schools, nurses/doctors, police officers. They travelled to conferences in the United States and eventually brought the Bridges program to BC. Due to stress she eventually gave this up

In the early years of her schizophrenia, I felt our relationship, on my part anyways, was one of "tolerance". Having to tolerate spending time with someone who had nothing to say. Someone who had no desire to do anything. We would talk on the phone everyday, if you could call it talking, mostly it was listening to each other breathe but I know it was her lifeline and it meant a lot to her to keep in touch with each of us even if only briefly each day.

Our relationship today is of reliance. Reliance on each other for different reasons. Our relationship is also of friendship. We have grown into friends. Our relationship is a mother/daughter relationship. She is still my mother, and I her daughter. Although at times, through necessity I become the mother and she the child. We have a bit of a psychic relationship as well. We think/say the same thing at the same time.

Before all of this and through all of it, she has been and continues to be a great mother, grandmother, sister, person, woman, and friend. I love her dearly. Tracy

My son is grown up now and he wrote a poem for me for Mother's Day, which I would like to share with you.

MY HERO

I was but a kid, when they took my mom away,
They said that she was sick and that she couldn't stay.
It seemed a dance of demons, had taken over her head,
I could not even imagine, the depth of my mother's dread.
I was not her fault, it's just the way it was
For three kids seeking answers, no comfort in 'just because'.
Doctors, meds and meetings, to find out what was wrong,
For Mom the time went slowly, it must have seemed so long.
In my mothers sleep, comfort she could find,
It seemed the only reprieve for her troubled mind.
In time she found the warrior, that in her lay within,
She said "you cannot have me, my soul you will not win".
I will fight and fight, of that you can be sure,
The love for my family is stronger and could not be more pure.
The journey has been a long one, of that she can attest,
The hard fought battle with demons, the weight lifted off her chest.
It does not matter how, the fact is she's all better,
I'm showing you I'm proud of you, in my little letter.

So, if the world needs a hero, do not look far and wide,
For if you are the underdog, Yvonne is on you side.

THE ROCKWELL LIFE... As I look back over the years of my life, especially my childhood, I can equate it to a Norman Rockwell painting. The first few years of my life were out in the municipality of Surrey...I remember only a few vague details. As a family, we moved to White Rock to care for my fathers ailing mother until she passed away in 1970. I looked at my parents the way most kids do. I looked for love, support and encouragement and of course protection. I never lacked for anything. I had enough food to eat, friends in the neighbourhood and of course the wonder of growing up with the Pacific Ocean in my front yard. Life could not be more perfect. I remember my father being a little harder to please than my mom; he seemed to be the disciplinarian in the family. I was threatened more than once with him pulling over the car to retrieve a "switch" out of the bush so to receive a sound beating... to teach me what... I don't remember. My mom was the soft, caring person. I do remember her having to pull rank with us on occasion but with a notable difference in the way she dealt with things. She was able to be soft and still make her point. My parents kept us involved with the things we were interested in. My sisters were into bowling and girl-type clubs while I was in soccer, baseball and weightlifting. I always enjoyed my chance to shine at my chosen sport in front of my parents approving eyes. Life was great...

SHIT HITS THE FAN.....I guess I did not know the troubles that were brewing in my family or my parent's marriage at the time, but I found out in a most distressful way in my fourteenth year. It was about suppertime and I was on the street in front of my home playing catch with a friend of mine. Neither of my parents had arrived home yet. When they did arrive, they arrived together in two separate cars. My mom did not say hello, but was crying as she ran into our home with my father in hot pursuit. Neither had said a word, but something was definitely amiss. I headed straight into the house to see what was the matter. In the home, I heard my dad yelling at my mom , pounding his fist on the bedroom wall and telling my mom to get out of the house. Imagine how that might have felt to experience that! My sisters and I all started to cry thinking, 'what the hell is going on?' At the time, it did not really matter except that our father "the disciplinarian" wanted our mother to leave the house and not come back. I did not know what had happened that day or prior, I only knew the security of a family foundation was now shaken and all this drama was surreal. I remember yelling at my dad to leave my mom alone (I don't think I had ever exerted any kind of emotion towards him). He took me outside and tried to calm my fears without any explanation of what had happened. It wasn't working.

THE NEXT FEW WEEKS....were all about my mom laying in bed all day every day and my dad coming home from work to yell at her. I guess he felt their bedroom was a soundproof fortress, so it did not take long to put the pieces together. We still had sleepovers at our home; maybe it was an attempt to have some normalcy in an upside down world. It wasn't long before friends knew family secrets. I guess in retrospect, our friends were as supportive as they could be, given their respective maturities

Days and months had gone by. My Mothers sickness was progressing. My father had moved out of the house. We had no idea of the demons that took up residence in Moms mind. I am sure there were signs that my Mom was getting progressively worse. I started spending more time at a neighbour's home. They were family friends, she was a psychiatric nurse. I remember telling her some of the goings on in my home hoping she might "take charge" and say Enough!! Why the Fuck was nobody doing anything? What the hell can I do? Under the circumstances, I did what a lot of teenagers might do; I turned inwards and adopted a "self-preservation" way of dealing with things.

I am ashamed to admit that I took advantage of a bad situation. My mom was very predictable at the time. She would sleep, sleep and sleep some more. I remember taking her 1975 Cougar XR-7 without permission, started some drinking, smoking pot and was having sex at the age of 14 with my then 13 year old girlfriend. I would take the car so I could pick up my friends and go mushroom picking in the next municipality...magic mushrooms that is. My father was living in an apartment at the time at the other end of town and would come by, it seemed, only to fight some more with my mom. So, I was not really caring about a lot of things at this point. My girlfriend Trisha was there for me, as was her family. Her mom had that intuition that knew I was hurting. That sentence just made me tear up!! She fed me and allowed me to sleep at their home on occasion if I needed to. As much as she helped me through a lot of bad, her hands were tied too. It's not like her parents and mine were friends, they were not...and I dated this girl for 4 years. My father ended up moving back into the home after a stint on his own. This was to be a failed attempt at reconciliation and still, my mom was not better. It's funny, the things you remember. My father had bought my mom a chequered green pant suit (this was still the 70's) and I remember my mom not liking it at all. I applaud his effort, but it was kind of hideous after all. I also remember my Dad having his nose out of joint because it was not my mothers taste in clothing.

Unbeknownst to us kids, my mother's family was having an intervention while we were at school. That was just as well. Never being one to get into fights at school, this was the day I had a fight in the school parking lot after school was out. Pent up rage allowed me to have the upper hand in the fight and I remember being sorry for breaking the other fellows nose. I ran all the way home, feeling crappy and ended up cutting my eye on a branch that was along the pathway that I walked home on. My eye was bleeding quite profusely. What a shitty day. Well, it got worse when I got home. My Dad was waiting to tell me what had happened and that my mom was being put into an institution across the Port Mann Bridge. A hard pill to swallow (pun intended) but at least something was to be done to help our mother…. It is not my intent to ramble as I remember events, but this drags up a lot of emotions and things I had let slide and tried to forget. Albeit, I find this a good exercise...

The first time I had ever heard of Crease Clinic was the day I had come home from school and my father had told me that's where my mom had been taken. Of course, I was shocked at the days events, but as I stated before, I was happy that something might finally be done about my moms condition. Imagine putting faith in people you had never met to cure your one and only mother of her demons. The word 'clinic' stuck in my mind as kind of a doctor's office type of place where everything was relatively sterile, magazine racks here and there and cheap art prints on the walls just to take up empty space between some neutral furniture. My first trip to Crease clinic was being driven there by my older sister with my mom's car. I am sure that my family may have driven by there once or twice not even noticing the place with the exception of some nicely manicured grounds alongside the highway. As my sisters and myself climbed up the stairs to this cement fortress for the first time, I remember being in awe of the size of the establishment.

I found it surprisingly clean inside. Nicely polished floors adorned the large foyer into the building. Up the stairs to the right was the nurses' station. A nurse had taken us down a corridor to the dreaded "day room" where my mom was. As we strolled down the hall, I could not believe the "crazies" in this place. People wailing and moaning, one slaps themselves, tongues hanging out, drooling, fucking awful I thought. Why is my mom in this place? My mom was waiting in the day room. How awkward is this? What the hell do I say, should I crack a joke to lighten the mood? It's like having an elephant in the room and no one is willing to state the obvious. I am relieved that she seems ok...downtrodden, but ok. She shows us the room where she has to sleep. Why did I notice to lock on her door? I am not feeling very good about this and I try to think that the doctors know best and do my best to ignore it. Other than having a down syndrome uncle on my fathers side, this is really my first experience with any kind of mental illness and such a facility. Back to the elephant in the room, I remember looking at all the people in the room with their various illnesses and behaviours almost making fun of them with my mom and sisters...ok...I still have a sense of humour and mom being here is a mere inconvenience for hopefully a very short time.

I was fascinated with a young fellow named David who did nothing but stare out the barred windows for hours on end hoping the creek across the road would flood and drown him in his sleep. Then there was Martha...poor old Martha, this woman had many strikes against her, but boy could she laugh which made us laugh...perhaps a silver lining in a very dark cloud. Maybe mom could kind of look out for her while she was there and give her some sense of purpose since nothing else made sense. After leaving Crease Clinic, my sisters and myself did not say much on the way home to White Rock

Death Friend

I have often referred to my mom as a warrior when talking about the battles she has faced in her life. Now that she is battling Cancer after having conquered Schizophrenia, I like to think that in a past life, my mother has agreed to take on two of the biggest demons in this life so that her children and grandchildren won't have to. Knowing how hard things have been for her, I do not know for sure if I would have the same strength as my mother. She has definitely been made from warrior stock. I also feel that her mothering and caring nature is a result from another great woman, my maternal grandmother more lovingly known as Mommom who was also very influential in my life

After partaking in the CIBC Run for the Cure in Vancouver, I had gone back to my sister's home to visit my Mom. It was a very good event and over 15,000 people involved. My Mom had asked me to shave her head as her hair was already starting to fall out. I lovingly obliged her request, laughing and joking all the way. I was hoping to allay my Moms fears by making her laugh when all I wanted to do was cry myself. I felt terrible because I did not want my Mom to have to endure any more hardship. She has since gotten herself a wig which seems to fit and look good for her. Mom takes all this in stride. I go back to my thoughts of her being a warrior, because I think she handles the situation better than myself.

Living in the Past.... As of late, my Mom and myself have been talking about past people, issues, memories, etc, all of them sparked by my Moms requests to have me make some audio CD's for her. It is all music from the past and brings back memories for me as well. After some rough teenage years with mom being ill, these songs trigger mostly good feelings for me than negative.

Regrets... Through a conversation with an aunt of mine quite recently, I found myself counselling her on the actions of her own teenager. The conversation forced me to look at myself as a teen and how terribly selfish I was. It brought back a memory of when my mom lived in Burnaby in a small apartment and any hospitalization at that point had not made much of a difference to her mental state. I would think nothing of calling her up from where I lived in White Rock to ask to borrow her car for the weekend. I thought little of her sitting all alone in her apartment for the weekend and more of myself having transportation for the weekend to do whatever the hell I wanted. I was a selfish teen going through my own stuff and cared about little else. I guess conversations, no matter who they are with and what they're about, you can find a lesson in them or find something to ponder. I found myself talking about responsibility and adulthood vs. teen years. There is no definitive line at which someone automatically grows up and is responsible. Some adults I know are still not there, I will find where I fit somewhere in the fray. To that end and despite some of the things I do, I like to think I am fairly well adjusted though opinions may vary.

Death Friend

I am quite happy to provide for my Mom this summation for her story. My regret is that one summary is grossly inadequate to describe the last 3 decades of her life. The brief scenarios I have described, as well as my sisters Tracy and Launa, do not come close to the amount of fear, anger, tears, incompetence by doctors, etc, etc. The list goes on. What I can tell you is that my Mom has come through a living hell and now wanting to share her story. For people who need a hero or for people who need to understand such things, it would be a good read indeed. I had stated before that I believe that my Mom had made an agreement in a previous life to take on the worst of the worst case scenarios in this life to spare her children and grandchildren the same fate.

Now as my Mom struggles through her Cancer ordeal, she has done so with a sense of humour and grace. No matter what she endures, she still sees the bright side of life and loves a good laugh. As she ages and other afflictions make themselves known to her body, she encompasses the saying...."Aging is not for sissies". My Mom has taught me a lot. I like to think fate has a lot to do with lessons we learn in life, such as where I ended up for a career. A career requiring compassion which I believe is an attribute from Mom. I am truly proud of her strength and poise as an individual that has faced life's greatest fears and come out with the ability to laugh. She would literally give you all she has to make you comfortable and suffer the hardship herself. That is just the way she is. You are a true warrior Mom. I love you very much and very proud of your accomplishments. You have touched many lives and people are richer for knowing you. Winston Churchill once said...."Difficulties mastered are opportunities won". The next stage of your life could definitely be your finest hour. All my love forever and always.....and forever proud of you.....Troy

Death Friend

My youngest daughter wrote a poem for me for Christmas when she was grown up. I will share it with you.

MY MOTHER, MY FRIEND

My Mother, my friend
Where would I be
Without you in my life

You share in my dark times
And rejoice in my bright
You're always there
When I just need some light

I'm thankful for you
You embrace all that's right
You're always there
Be it day or night

There's nothing I can't say
You just have a way
Of making my world better
From day to day

I'm thankful for you
You have such a grace
If there were more of you in the world
It would truly be
A much better place

All my love

THROUGH THE EYES OF BABES

My name is Launa and I am the baby of the family. I recall most of the same events as my sister and brother, but chronologically, for me they are quite mixed up.

I think I was 10 or 11 when my parent's marital problems started. I remember waking up about an hour or two after going to bed to my sister sobbing. I asked her why she was crying, but before she could answer I heard for myself. We could hear our dad yelling, our mom crying. We didn't know what to do, but eventually went downstairs to try and comfort our mother. This happened many more times until it seemed, there was nothing left of our family but him yelling, her crying, and us kids upset, confused and afraid of what was happening to our once happy family.

Things took a turn for the worse for my mom. Her sorrow had become so immense that she could no longer get out of bed and all she could do was cry. At least this is what I could see from my eleven year old perspective. I didn't know that something bigger had moved in and taken up residence in her mind. It seemed as though her brown eyes had turned to black. There was such a profound void in her that nothing could satiate. Not even her children and we tried desperately. Our mother was the glue that held us together, she was our nurturer and caregiver our emotional stability. And then, she told us that she didn't want to live anymore.

My world as I knew it had completely crumbled from its foundation. I was lost. I felt so alone and so scared. So scared, that my mom would take her own life and leave me. I couldn't understand what evil forces had now caused so much havoc in our lives. I was, however, starting to realize my mom was not just sad, she was sick. I remember being angry at my father because it seemed to me, be I right or wrong, that he blamed my mother for her illness. You can no more blame her for having schizophrenia than you can someone for having M.S. or epilepsy.

It is very difficult to sit here and write all of this down. It is through a sea of tears that I am reliving each of these memories. I am surprised, that at 42, the nerve is still so raw. The hardest thing for me is to share this with my mom because I have spend my whole fife trying to protect her from knowing how it has affected me, I never wanted her to know because it's not her fault. I have never once blamed her. In fact she is the bravest person I know. She has fought more demons time and time again and come out victorious every time. She has more integrity and more courage of conviction that any other person I know. I am proud to say she is my mom! She has taught me to be a fighter and to never give up. She had led by example even when she had absolutely no idea anyone was watching.

I have been through three sets of counselling, throughout my life and the last and most intense was only a mere four years ago. At 38 years old I was finally diagnosed with post traumatic stress disorder, and a wonderful lady named Sarah finally helped me to break down most of the walls that have held me captive most of my life. The quality of my life is the best it's ever been. I feel like a whole person, something I have searched for my entire adult life. I have learned how to play and my inner child for the first time, I believe, is happy. I have searched and searched to find some sanctuary, some peace of mind, and I finally found it in me! It was always there; I just couldn't see or feel it.

I believe I was 14 when my mom was committed to Crease Clinic at Riverview hospital. To me it was a horrible, scary place that seemed like a prison. The rooms were like cells, with locks and bars on the windows. How could anyone actually get better in a place like this? I thought. I felt helpless and hopeless for my mom for me for my sister and brother. I saw things in that hospital that I never want to see again. There was, however, a bright spot or two in this cement hell. There was Martha, who despite all of her problems and disabilities, would make us laugh and consequently the entire room would get going. Then there was the piano lady who could play the piano so beautifully that everyone in the room would start to cry. Despite all the madness in there and yet still undiagnosed, my mom did make some progress and was finally released.

Crease Clinic was not the only hospital my mom had a stint in, but it certainly left a lasting impression that has forever haunted my mind.

During these young years of my life, I did meet a lady whom had moved in just down the back lane from our family home. She was a single mother of two girls, one the same age as me. The other a couple of years younger. My older sister had actually started babysitting these two girls. It so happened that the older girl was in my class at school and we started to get to know each other a little bit. I started to spend a lot of time at their house as Janie got to know me and what was happening in my family, she took me in under her wing and gave me guidance, understanding and nurturing as if I was her daughter too. She could barely afford to house, clothes and feed her own two girls, yet she had no problems housing and feeding me when I needed it. She has loved me and cared for me like I was her own and for the past 30 years Janie and her two daughters, Deanna and Anita have been a part of my family and me a part of theirs. For which my mom and I will be eternally grateful for their love and support over the years

We lost Janie just over a year ago in a tragic accident. I will and do miss her greatly. She was a mother, a friend and a confidante, and in many ways, she saved my life.

I started to run amok at 12. I started smoking cigarettes, I would drink alcohol if I could get my hands on it, and in the next year or so I would smoke pot too, if I could get my hands on that also. I guess escaping reality was what I was after. Janie could see what I was up to and as much as she knew she couldn't stop me, she would talk to me and ask questions about why I was doing, what I was doing. She kept her eye on me and just always let me know that she cared. I eventually got a lot of my destructive behaviour under control Janie was the only one that knew at that time what demons I was conquering.

Our father was doing a lot of dating at this time and was spending a lot of time with his girlfriends and their families. My oldest sister had become our primary caregiver in the home. She was doing most of the cooking, cleaning, etcetera. And when she started working, she would also give my brother and I money when we needed it. We relied on her and she would always help us where she could.

I, like my mother, have become a survivor of my demons. Fighting them has proved to be the most successful and beneficial thing I will ever do. I know I have everything I need, in me, to face my fears and rise above them. This I learned from my mom.

CONCLUSION

My boyfriend of 22 years, retired in 2005. He was diagnosed with cancer of the lungs and bone in January 2007. I moved back in with him and looked after him, which was a struggle and stressful as he was on Morphine and was very confused. He did not last to long as he passed away in September. Life has been very stressful and lonely without him.

I have 3 children, 6 grandchildren and 3 great grandchildren, so I have a lot to live for. I will keep busy with my writing and painting. I have been diagnosed with breast cancer in June 2008. Had my right breast removed in July and now I am having chemo treatments, which can be some rough days to it. I will have three months of chemo and then put on pills for a year, hopefully that will cure it.

If this story has been interesting and educational, I am certainly pleased to present it. It may help some people to know that when you have a diagnose of a mental illness it is still possible to live quite a normal life, if you can find the medications with the least side effects. Thank you for taking the time to read my story, and I hope it was helpful to some. There is always HOPE.

Help Our People Endure

LaVergne, TN USA
05 January 2010
168975LV00001B/15/P